ROBERT A. HARRIS

ELEGY FOR THE TIME OF CHANGE

MUSIC DEPARTMENT

OXFORD
UNIVERSITY PRESS

Composer's Note

Elegy for the Time of Change, composed in June 2020, is in part a reaction to the horrific death of George Floyd, who was murdered as the entire world witnessed his cruel suffocation by a police officer. Floyd was forced to the ground and struggled to breathe for 9 minutes and 29 seconds—calling out for his mother—before taking his last breath and dying. The impetus for writing this piece was a sermon delivered shortly after this lamentable event by the Rev. Michael Curry, Presiding Bishop and Primate of the Episcopal Church. In that sermon, Bishop Curry delivered words of solace, love, and the hope that the United States, struggling with polarization, mistrust, and disparity, might come together as a unified nation of brotherhood, peace, and equality. Most moving and memorable were his recurring references to words of the spiritual *There is a Balm in Gilead*. Those words of assurance, woven into his beautifully crafted sermon, were the real inspiration for *Elegy*, which I began to write immediately after the sermon's conclusion. Brief musical quotes from the spiritual occur throughout the piece, representing the aspiration that we as a people will soon unite, revive our collective spirits, and heal the wounded, sin-sick soul of our nation.

In Memoriam ...

Tanisha Anderson, Sandra Bland, Rayshard Brooks, Michael Brown, Philando Castile, Stephon Clark, Michelle Cusseaux, George Floyd, James Floyd, Janisha Fonville, Eric Garner, Freddie Gray, Akai Gurley, Justin Howell, Botham Jean, Atatiana Jefferson, Trayvon Martin, Sean Monterrosa, Gabriella Nevarez, Tamir Rice, Aura Rosser, Alton Sterling, Breonna Taylor
et al. ...

In Memoriam …

Elegy for the Time of Change

ROBERT A. HARRIS

Sw.: Strings 8'
Gt.: Foundations 8', Sw. to Gt.
Ch.: Foundations 8'
Ped.: Foundations 16', 8', Sw. to Ped.

Somewhat slowly (♩ = 63–66)

Printed in Great Britain

OXFORD UNIVERSITY PRESS, MUSIC DEPARTMENT, GREAT CLARENDON STREET, OXFORD OX2 6DP

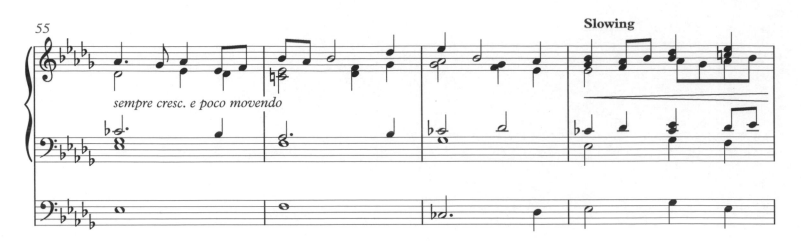